MW01128347

Daylon,

May your piggybank
never go empty!

Love Author
Cuptal
McL

HARMONEY
& THE EMPTY PIGGY BANK

by Crystal D. McLean

illustrations & design by
Dave Lentz
& Rob Simmons

Published by Parker & Co. Press, LLC

P.O. Box 50040

Richmond, VA 23250

Library of Congress Control
Number: 2020915412

ISBN: 978-1-7355610-0-4 (E-book)

ISBN: 978-1-7355610-1-1 (Hardback)

ISBN: 978-1-7355610-2-8 (Paperback)

Dedication Page

To Abba, who I can do all things through.

To the real Harmony, my daughter, who inspired the creative, spunky, smart, and full-of-life character in this story. I love you, princess.

To my husband, my biggest supporter. I love you!

And to my "Village," you know who you are! Thank you for the push!

In Loving Memory of Granny Hal, Aunt Brenda, Uncle Anthony, Grandaddy Leon, and "Papa"! Your legacy lives on!

Helping You Understand

There may be a few words that you may not understand as you are reading. To help you, these words and their meanings are listed below:

- Allowance: An amount of money paid to someone on a regular basis

- Budget: A plan that shows you how to spend, share, or save your money

- Business: An organization where people work together to make and sell products or offer services

- Charity: An organization set up to raise money to help those in need

- Customer: A person who buys goods or services from a business

- Donation: A gift someone gives to a cause they believe in or to someone in need

- Earning: To receive money in return for labor or a service

- Entrepreneur: Someone who sets up their own business

- Goods: Items that are bought (such as food, clothes, toys, shoes, and much more)

- Inventory: Supplies needed in order to make goods and offer services

- Organization: A group of people formed together for a specific purpose

- Product: An item offered for sale

- Saving: Putting money aside for a purpose or a plan

- Service: An action someone does for someone else that can be paid for (like a haircut or teeth cleaning)

- Spend: To pay money to buy a good or service

- Tip: Extra money given to someone as a reward for good service

- Value: The importance or worth of something

Table of Contents:

Chapter 1: Girls' Day Out.………………………....………..1

Chapter 2: The Long Ride Home.………………………..…..6

Chapter 3: Dad's Home.………………………………....….10

Chapter 4: Different Day, Same Disappointment.….....15

Chapter 5: The Presentation.………………………....….…21

Chapter 6: Plan in Motion.……………………………....…25

Chapter 7: Where are All the People?..........................31

My Guided Journal.……………………………….....……….38

My Money Journal.……………………………….....……….39

Granny Hal's Famous Lemonade Recipe..…...……..…...41

Ooey Gooey Cookies Recipe.……………………....……...42

Chapter 1:
Girls' Day Out

It's a beautiful, sunny day, and Harmoney and Mom are going out for their usual Girls' Day Out. Every week, her and Mom take this moment to bond and talk. They liked to talk about school, new songs, gymnastics, and everything in between. Some days, they grabbed ice cream, and other days, they went shopping.

As Harmoney rides in the car with Mom, she thinks of what she is going to get today. Will it be some candy, lip gloss, or maybe even headphones? She got excited just thinking about it.

In that moment, as Mom drove out of neighborhood, Harmoney saw her friends laughing, singing, and riding their bikes. She silently wondered when she would finally have her chance to be a part of the fun. She really wanted a bike but had not spoken to her parents about it yet. Harmoney thought about how much fun she would have riding one.

Harmoney loves the shopping trips, but today seems extra special. She likes how sunny it is, and how much fun her and Mom are having in the car today. Normally, Mom leads the songs, even though her singing is not the best. Today, Mom let Harmoney lead the songs. Maybe she is tired of Harmoney laughing at her in the back seat when she sings the wrong notes or forgets the words to the song.

Harmoney began to wonder where they were going today. Mom is known for keeping the location a surprise. Harmoney thought, "Maybe one day, Mom will let me plan the field trip," as she finished leading her favorite song!

Harmoney was deep in her note, singing with her eyes closed, when she felt the car stop.

"We are here!" Mom screeched.

Today, they ended up at the mall. Harmoney giggled and was excited since it had been a while. Harmoney jumped out, smiling. This is one of her favorite places in the world. She loved how there were so many different stores, and so much stuff to buy! She was super happy and she kept the singing spree going.

Harmoney danced up and down the mall, looking at all of the stores, singing her own made-up song. "I am awesome! I am fly! I am beautiful! Don't you know why?"

While turning the corner, admiring all the nice items, the most AMAZING thing caught her eye in the middle of the mall! At that moment, Harmoney stopped singing. There she stood, gazing at the most beautiful thing she had ever seen! A BIKE! Not just any bike, but the bike she had seen on many commercials, and some of her friends had it. Before her eyes was the LoMax 10 Bicycle, the newest, latest model. It had a blingy basket where she could put her phone and other stuff. She started to play with the display bike and wondered how she would look with it.

Mom walked over to Harmoney and noticed that she was sitting on the bike. Harmoney was in a daze imagining herself riding with her friends, racing against them, listening to music from her iPod while riding, and so much more.

Mom snapped her out of her daydream. "Earth to Harmoney!"

Immediately, Harmoney came back to reality. She shrieked, "Mom, I have to have it! Please, Mom? Please? May I have it? PRETTY PLEASE?"

Mom placed her finger on Harmoney's mouth and said, "Calm down, and tell me what all this fuss is about. What do you have to have, sweetie?"

Harmoney tried to use her inside voice, but her excitement caused her to jump and yell, "Mom, this! This right here! Isn't it beautiful?

You KNOW how bad I want a bike, and this one is perfect! I can do so much with this, and some of my friends have one like this. But this one is so much prettier. Look at the sparkly pegs!" Harmoney smiled. She just knew Mom was buying this bike for her today!

"Harmoney, remember how Dad and I have been talking to you about saving up for the things you want?" Mom asked, crossing her arms.

"Yes, Mom, but remember I saved and used all of that money for my hoverboard 3 months ago." Harmoney let out a disappointed sigh. "Besides, Mom, it takes so long to save that much money."

Glancing from the bike to the floor, then back at Mom, Harmoney whined and asked, "Could you please get this for me today, and I can save for my helmet later? I will do extra chores and I will be responsible-"

Mom interrupted with, "No, sweetie. I am sorry. I understand how much you want this bike. However, you must remember what we taught you. If you save up for the things you want, you will appreciate them more, and learn the value of saving and earning. Now, let's get home for dinner."

Harmoney huffed, rolled her eyes, and blurted out, "But Mom, it's only $150, and it will take me FOREVER to save that much! It's really not that much money for you and Dad. Please, Mom?"

Mom said firmly, "Harmoney, I meant what I said. Money does not grow on trees, bushes, or in gardens. You have to work for it. Now, let's go grab our favorite cookies and crème ice cream, and go home for dinner."

Chapter 2:
The Long Ride Home

Normally, after a Girls' Day Out, the ride home is filled with singing, girl talk, and playing the competitive game of Punch Buggy. Not this time. Today's ride home was quiet. Harmoney did not feel like singing. She felt more like crying. She had her heart set on that bike.

Mom could have bought it for her, but instead, she said, "No." That "no" hurt her feelings. Harmoney felt that she was a good girl. She always did her best to follow the rules at home and at school.

She looked out the window with a sad face. To make matters worse, while going home, they passed two of her same friends still riding their bikes in the neighborhood and laughing. They looked happy, and Harmoney couldn't help but get even sadder that she could not be a part of it.

Mom watched Harmoney silently. She knew Harmoney wanted the bike, but she also knew there was an important lesson in telling her no. Focused on the open road ahead and her sad daughter in the backseat, she couldn't help but remember learning the same lesson around Harmoney's age. She wanted a VX 2000, the newest video game system. Yet, the answer was also no from her parents.

She wanted to somehow make her daughter feel better but couldn't think of the words to say. She knew Harmoney would someday learn the important lesson, and she could not help but wonder how long it would take.

***

After Mom parked in the driveway, without a word, Harmoney jumped out of the car, went inside, and ran upstairs to her room. Harmoney plopped on her bed and couldn't get the thought of the bike out of her head. She turned to her dresser and noticed her piggy bank. With high hopes, she hopped off the bed and picked up the purple glass pig. She shook it, heard the loud, rattling sound of coins, and thought, "It doesn't sound like $150." Yet, she stayed positive. Harmoney squeezed her eyes shut, hoping for a miracle as she twisted the secret opening at the bottom and peeked inside. She saw four one-dollar bills, two quarters, and seven pennies. "$4.57. Really? That's all I have? How can I buy a bike with this?" She whined.

"My parents are always telling me, 'No to this and No to that,'" she mumbled. "Don't they get it? I am the only one who does not have a bike." Harmoney slammed her door, stomped back to the bed, and buried her face in the pillow, soaking it with tears.

Chapter 3:
Dad's Home

Harmoney was still sobbing when she heard the front door open, and Dad coming in. She wiped away her tears and thought to herself excitedly, "Maybe there is still a chance!"

Harmoney jumped off the bed and ran downstairs to greet Dad. In her happiest and sweetest voice, she exclaimed, "Dad! Dad! My favorite person in the whole wide world!" She skipped to Dad and hugged him tightly.

Dad laughed. "Hey, princess, how are you? Wow, what did I do to deserve so much extra love from you today?" Harmoney leaned on his shoulders and hugged his neck tightly, with Dad returning the embrace.

Harmoney is truly a daddy's girl, but Dad also knows Harmoney. While he was enjoying the moment, he was also trying to figure out what was coming next. His princess wanted something; he just didn't know what. Harmoney acted the same way when she wanted the hoverboard.

"Well, since you asked, let's go into the living room to talk about that. We don't want anyone to hear us," she said in a whisper while looking in Mom's direction.

Mom glanced over, then went back to cooking. She chuckled under her breath, seeing how serious her daughter was. She always loved how her daughter never gave up on the things she wanted.

Once seated, Harmoney hugged Dad again, then looked up at him, smiling. He saw the innocent look in her eyes and asked, "What happened? Did you break Mom's jewelry again?"

She quickly turned to Mom to make sure she didn't hear, then looked back at Dad. "No, Dad! I learned my lesson the last time. This time, it's something different and more important."

Dad tilted his head to match Harmoney's. "Princess, what is it?" Dad asked.

"Dad, you always tell me how much you love me, right? You love me to infinity, right? You tell me there is nothing you won't do to make sure I know that I am safe, happy, and loved, right?" Dad's forehead was wrinkled in concentration as he nodded his head in agreement.

"All of my friends have bikes. I am the only one who doesn't. I really want to be able to ride around the neighborhood with them. Since you really love me, can I pleeeeeaaasseee get this bike? I saw one at the store, and it was just PERFECT for me! It even had a sparkly, glittery, shiny basket where I can put my iPod and stuff. And guess what? It was my favorite color. Dad, you do know what my favorite color is, don't you?"

Dad exclaimed, "Of course I know your favorite color. It's purple!"

Harmoney smiled from ear to ear and gave Dad a high five. "So, Dad, can I get the bike I saw today? I want to get it before anyone else does." Looking at him with those baby doll eyes, she awaited her "yes" from Dad. She was already doing a happy dance when she heard Dad respond.

"Sweetie, how much is this perfect, shiny bike?"

While still dancing, she had the price memorized and stated, "Dad, it only costs $150."

Harmoney was still waiting on her "yes" when Dad asked, "What did Mom say about this?" His princess stopped dancing, the twinkle in her eyes disappearing as she remembered her talk with Mom. "I know you remember when we talked to you before about saving your money for the things you want, right?"

Harmoney nodded her head. She couldn't say anything. Harmoney was confused. She just knew this plan would've worked.

Dad continued, "Let me remind you that, yes, you did save your money, but you made the choice to spend it all on the hoverboard you wanted."

Harmoney turned to walk away and said, "Never mind, Dad. Just forget it. May I go to my room, please?"

Dad firmly responded, "Yes, for a moment, then go wash your hands and get ready for dinner."

Harmoney went back to her room, even sadder than before. She washed up for dinner, went downstairs, and struggled to eat her food. She just couldn't understand why her parents were acting this way. Dinner was silent, like the car ride home.

Mom finally broke the silence. "Harmoney, it's not that we don't love you, but we really want to make sure you are responsible enough to have a bike. We also want you to remember you have to save up for the things you want. Just keep doing your chores and getting your allowance, and pretty soon, you may be able to buy your own bike."

Harmoney sadly responded, "Yes ma'am," and nodded. She felt even more hopeless.

Chapter 4:
Different Day,
Same Disappointment

The next day, Harmoney got dressed for school and started adding things up in her mind. She earns $15 each week for her allowance.

"If I save up with my allowance, it will actually take 10 weeks," she thought. "Ten weeks equals 70 days. It might as well be forever." She put her head down at the thought of it.

The thought of 70 days, 1,680 hours, was too long for her. What if someone else buys that bike? It was the only one on display with that color! What if the store closes for good?

As she was getting ready for school, she grew gloomier by the moment. She headed out for school in slow motion, trying to wrap her mind around everything that had happened the day before.

The bus ride to school was normally fun. But today, Harmoney looked out the bus window with her head pressed to the glass, not interested in talking to anyone.

Harmoney went through the school day with the same mood. The lunch bell blared loudly, and she realized the day was halfway over.

Harmoney's best friend, Ava, came and sat with her in the cafeteria. When Ava looked at her friend, she saw how unhappy and upset she was.

"Harmoney, what's wrong with you? You have been looking sad all day. You didn't even laugh when Jeff tripped over his book bag earlier. Now that was funny!" Ava chuckled.

Harmoney looked at Ava and blurted out, "Ava, my parents don't want me to have any fun. They want me to keep doing chores, making good grades in school, saving my allowance, and making wise decisions. And then, when I ask for something, they tell me, 'No!' They say, 'You have to earn it. You have to work for it.' Blah, blah, blah." Harmoney held back tears as she remembered yesterday's conversation.

Ava looked at her and asked, "So, um, what did you ask for?"

"I only asked for a bike. A bike, Ava! A bike, so I can ride around the neighborhood with my friends! I am the only one who can't. It only costs $150. I even planned to do extra chores. They still said, 'No!' I am not old enough to get a job. How am I supposed to earn that much money?" Harmoney whined.

Ava chimed in, "Yeah, I can see why you are sad. My uncle Anthony gave me my first bike for Christmas. OOH! Maybe you will get one for Christmas!"

Harmoney turned and looked at Ava in disbelief with her eyes wide and mouth open. "CHRISTMAS? Ava, I cannot wait until Christmas. That is longer than me saving for 10 weeks. There has got to be a better way." The girls were so deep in thought they forgot about their lunch getting cold.

Harmoney remembered her Granny Hal and her famous lemonade. When Harmoney was younger, Granny Hal would always make it for the entire neighborhood, and they loved it. Before Granny Hal passed away, she had taken the time to teach Harmoney how to make it herself. This was something Harmoney would always hold dear to her.

Suddenly, Harmoney shook Ava's shoulders and exclaimed, "Ava, I got it! I got it! I got it!"

Ava asked anxiously, "Well? What is it? Tell me, tell me!"

"I can make Granny's Famous Lemonade and sell it. That way, I can earn the money for my bike, and it won't take forever!" The girls hugged and celebrated Harmoney's great idea.

Ava got inspired after their embrace and said, "Wait a minute. What if you get your mom to help you make some of her 'Ooey Gooey' cookies? You remember, the ones she made for the slumber party. They were so, so good!" Ava rubbed her tummy thinking about the delicious cookies.

"I am going to show Mom and Dad that I am serious. After they see my plan, I think they will love it!" Harmoney was so excited she hugged Ava again and said, "This is why you are my best friend! You always know what to say to make my day!"

Ava giggled. "That rhymed!"

Harmoney rushed home and finished her homework in record time. She then went straight to work on her presentation. She grabbed a poster board, markers, crayons, glitter, and pencils. First, she scribbled her plan down on a piece of paper. She scribbled and erased repeatedly until she was satisfied with her final project. She wrote down the recipe for the lemonade, then drew cups and dollar signs. She also drew pictures of Mom's cookies and a piggy bank. After that, she carefully sketched a 3-D rectangle and wrote the words "REFRESHMENTS FOR SALE" on it.

Harmoney could hardly contain her excitement. She was so proud of herself. She hid the poster in her closet. She planned to present it to her parents the next day. Harmoney prayed, then drifted off to sleep, thinking of the refreshment stand and her cute, brand new bicycle.

Chapter 5:
The Presentation

The next morning, Harmoney's alarm clock rang and she woke up excited. Today was presentation day! She was so excited that she got dressed ahead of her usual time. Harmoney grabbed her presentation poster and rushed downstairs. Her parents were in the kitchen doing their usual morning routine. Dad was sitting at the table, watching the sports channel, while Mom was cooking breakfast.

Harmoney strutted into the kitchen. "Good morning, my AWESOME parents!"

They looked at each other, not knowing what to think of their bright-eyed and cheery daughter. She is usually not a morning person.

"Well, good morning to you, too. What's got you so excited this morning?" Mom asked, waiting for an explanation.

Dad asked jokingly, "Who are you, and what have you done with my daughter?" They all laughed.

Harmoney cleared her throat. "Mom and Dad, I apologize for acting like a brat yesterday. I thought about what you said, and I think I have the perfect idea to earn the money for my bike." Harmoney was beaming with confidence. Her parents were eager to hear her idea. Dad muted the TV, and Mom turned around to listen attentively.

"For the next five weeks, I want to save my allowance, build a refreshment stand, and call it 'Granny's Treats.' I want to make Granny Hal's Famous Lemonade that everyone loves. And Mom, your 'Ooey Gooey' cookies are sure to be a bestseller. I want to sell the lemonade and cookie combo for $3."

Harmoney smiled and continued, "Ava has agreed to help me with the flyers and running the stand. If I make enough, I hope to buy the bike on my own, give Ava some money for helping, buy some toys for kids who are less fortunate, and put the rest in my piggy bank. And I am going to need my parents' help! Could you both help me, please?" Her eyes twinkled with joy as she nervously awaited their answer.

No one made a sound. Mom had her hand over her mouth in awe, and Dad barely blinked.

Harmoney finally belted out, "Um, so what do you think?"

Mom came over and picked her up. "Harmoney, I am so proud of you. You took the time to think about all of this on your own. This makes us so happy. I honestly don't know what else to say." She hugged Harmoney as she fought back tears, thinking of how much she had grown in just a few days.

Dad stood up and joined the embrace. "Now, this is what I call growing up. Baby girl, we will support you all the way. Just remember, you have to keep doing your chores in order to keep getting your full allowance."

She boldly replied, "Dad, I have already planned to do my chores every morning before school, and every night before bed." Dad nodded proudly.

It was at that point that they had their moment. It was not a Mom and Harmoney moment. It was not a Dad and Harmoney moment. It was a family moment. There were hugs, love, and a kitchen full of joy, and the smell of pancakes, of course. Harmoney could not have been happier.

Chapter 6:
Plan in Motion

The time had come to carry out Harmoney's plan. Harmoney was true to her word. She got up early every morning to do her chores and tidied up right after school and before bed to earn her allowance. Meanwhile, she and Ava worked on flyers for the big event. They posted the flyers at school and in the neighborhood and told all their friends about the sale. Harmoney told the mailman, Mr. Ernest, the garbage truck men, and anyone else she happened to run into.

"I want everyone to come! You won't be disappointed!" She said to them excitedly.

Five weeks later, and after completing her chores, she earned all of her allowance. Harmoney now had $75 saved up to get the supplies for the Granny's Treats refreshment sale.

Harmoney remembered saving for her hoverboard 3 months ago. But this time was different because she came up with a plan that involved others. She had planned and presented. And now, she was preparing to make it happen. With all the support from her family and friends, Harmoney felt good about her idea. She was sure this would be a success and couldn't wait for the big day to come.

***

Harmoney and Mom were on another Girls' Day Out. But this day was all about preparation. The sale day was near, and she wanted to make sure everything was ready. Mom had taken care of making the shopping list for Harmoney since she knew both of the recipes by heart: Lemons, limes, and sugar for the lemonade, and all the ingredients for the "Ooey Gooey" cookies.

Not only did Harmoney have to buy ingredients, she also had to purchase supplies, like cups, straws, tablecloths, napkins, bags to place the cookies in, stickers for the labels, a box to keep the money safe, and a notebook to keep track of the inventory.

When they got to the register, the cashier rang up everything and said, "Your total is $71.50." Harmoney's eyes grew wide in shock as she gave the cashier the money.

As they left the store, Harmoney said, "Mom, this is a lot of work. I did not know it would cost this much to get what I needed. Almost all of my allowance is gone."

Mom hugged her tired shopping partner and said, "Sweetie, you have to spend money in order to make money. Business is all about making sure you have prepared properly. The goal is to make more money than you spent." Harmoney sighed and nodded her head in agreement, too tired to complain.

Harmoney and Mom got in the car and headed home. They were tired, but they still managed to sing. Harmoney was so tired, she let Mom lead the song this time. Mom forgot some of the words, as always, so they laughed the whole way home.

The next day, the time had come to see if their hard work was really going to pay off. Harmoney and Mom had spent the day before mixing, cutting, baking, and bagging cookies.

Some of the flour was tossed in the air, and Harmoney ended up looking like a ghost. Dad came in and saw the chaos and started taking pictures while laughing. Ava came over later to help make the lemonade. There was quite a bit of measuring, pouring, and mixing.

Harmoney and Ava did a lemon challenge video with the leftover lemons to show their expressions after eating them. Dad laughed as he recorded the silliness. After that, everyone helped make the labels and the price list.

Harmoney kept asking the same questions anxiously. "Mom, do you think anybody will come? Mom, are the cookies gooey enough? Mom, is the lemonade too sweet?"

Mom finally said, "Listen, sweetie, you have done such a great job. You planned and prepared, and we are so proud of you. You and Ava have told so many people about today. Dad and I have shared with our friends, family, and coworkers. Let's just see how great today will be. Now run outside and see if your dad needs any help."

When Harmoney went outside, she was excited to see Dad standing next to a booth with the words "Granny's Treats" painted on the front. She screamed, hugged him, and thanked him for the surprise.

The smell of cookies traveled throughout the neighborhood. Granny's Treats was officially in business.

Chapter 7:
Where are All the People?

Ava ran up to Harmoney. They hugged, excited and ready for the big day. Ava said, "I will help you pass out cookies, and mark down how many we sell."

"Thank you, Ava! That is why you are my best friend. I am so glad you are here with me today." Harmoney smiled and yelled, "Let's get this party started!"

The girls sat in the booth. Ava counted the cookie bags, and Harmoney counted the cups and straws. Harmoney looked down both ends of the street. There was no one in sight. The flyer said the event started at 2:00 p.m. It was 2:06.

Mom stood on the porch and watched the girls. Harmoney asked Ava with a disappointed tone, "Ava, do you think people forgot? Did I say the wrong day?" She was worried. "Where are all the peop-?"

HONK! HONK! She heard the garbage truck coming down the street. Harmoney jumped into action. She tied her apron and got ready for the task ahead.

Before the garbage men got there, their first customer, Mrs. Brenda, walked up. She was one of the sweetest people Harmoney knew and was also Granny Hal's best friend.

GRANNY'S TREATS

Mrs. Brenda took a sip of lemonade, then exclaimed, "Wow, Harmoney! Your lemonade tastes just like your Granny Hal's. This is so good! Can I get a picture with you two? I want to remember this day!"

"Yes ma'am!" Harmoney and Ava said in unison as they jumped up with huge smiles for a selfie with Mrs. Brenda.

"Girls, thank you, and remember to always reach for your dreams. You can do anything you put your mind to," Mrs. Brenda said, hugging them both and adding a tip to the jar.

"Thank you, Mrs. Brenda," they both said, enjoying the embrace.

The orders really started rolling in after that. Harmoney was pouring and handing out lemonade as Ava handed out cookies. It felt like everyone in the neighborhood came to see what Granny's Treats was all about.

AVA, MRS. BRENDA, + ME!

Harmoney could not believe her eyes. Not only did almost all the neighbors come, but some of her friends from school and even some people from Dad's job showed up. Those who came were delighted to see two young girls working so hard. Harmoney and Ava were sure to say, "Thank you!" to everyone as they sold the items. Mom overheard different customers talking about how good the cookies were, and how tasty the lemonade was. It was indeed a great day

Everyone's order was filled quickly, and no customer was left unhappy. Ava handed out the last order and looked down at her tally notebook. She realized they had completely sold out and had served over 80 people!

They were too tired to jump for joy. So, the girls just plopped in their chairs and waved their hands instead. Mom and Dad helped the girls clean up.

Harmoney tugged Mom's arm and said in a soft voice, "Mom, that was hard work."

Mom smiled. "You girls did so amazing! I am so proud of you both. Now let's see how your hard work has paid off!" The girls wiped their brows as they headed inside.

After all the cleaning was done, and everything was back in its place, they all went into the kitchen, where Mom placed all the money on the table.

"Let's count and see how much you've earned," Mom said.

Harmoney remembered how Mom taught her to count the money. "Twenty-dollar bills first, ten-dollar bills second, five-dollar bills third, and one-dollar bills last," she recited.

33

After all the bills were counted, they counted the coins. Harmoney's eyes grew wide in disbelief. She could not believe the total amount. She almost wanted to ask Mom to count it all again! From the sales, tips, and donations, Harmoney had earned $322.50. She was so overjoyed! She hugged and thanked Mom.

"Oh, my goodness, Mom! This is more than enough. I have enough to buy my bike. I can ride with my friends now!" Harmoney yelled. Ava joined in the celebration. They laughed and danced. Dad walked in smiling and started dancing, too. "We did it! We did it!" They all cheered together.

Mom cleared her throat. "Harmoney, sweetie, I am so proud of you. But remember, it matters how you spend it. Let's create a plan."

The dance party was over, and it was back to business. Harmoney grabbed a piece of paper and began to write down how she planned to spend her earnings.

Mom told her, "Now that you know what you want to buy, let's budget how much it is going to cost."

Everyone knew the bike was the first item on the list. The bike would cost $150.

"Out of $322.50, after you purchase the bike, you will have $172.50 left," Dad said.

Harmoney and her parents decided to give Ava $50 because she worked extra hard to help with the event. Harmoney now had $122.50 left to spend. Mom suggested she put aside $35 to buy small toys to donate to other children. After everything on her list was budgeted, Harmoney still had $87.50 to put in her piggy bank for savings. Harmoney was glad she had a lot more than $4 in her piggy bank this time. She laughed thinking about it. She even started thinking about how she could use this money and grow it even more.

Harmoney looked at her parents and Ava with excitement, knowing that she accomplished a lot. "It looks like I am getting that purple, glittery, sparkly, shiny bike sooner than I thought!" She smiled and started jumping. Not only was she getting her bike, but she also had earned enough money to help others.

"This was the best day ever! Now, let's go and get my new bike!"
Harmoney ran out the door and to the car.

The next day, after riding her bike for the first time with her
friends, Harmoney sat on the front porch smiling and thought, "I really
did it." The neighbors and other customers were still talking about
how good the lemonade and cookies were. Since things went so well,
Harmoney asked her parents if she could do the sale again. They said
yes. Granny's Treats was now in business for the long haul!

Harmoney learned some valuable lessons. She now understood what it meant to work hard for the things she wants. She no longer pouted when her parents told her no. She realized that the art of managing money is for all ages.

Harmoney wasn't the only one who learned lessons about budgeting, saving, and charity. Ava learned some lessons, too, and she was eager to help with future sales. This time, the two best friends set goals together. One of their goals was to make a difference by helping others!

- How can you work hard to make a difference?

My Guided Money Journal

I am talented at: _____

My favorite hobby is: _____

If I had the money, I would buy: _____

This costs (how much): $ _____

With my parent's permission, I will use my
_____ talent and create
a plan that will help me to earn money in order to
buy _____, which costs
$_____. I plan to earn extra so I can donate/give to
_____ (person/organization).

After reading this book, what did you learn about money?

_____

_____

What else would you like to learn about money?

_____

_____

I plan to ask my parent or guardian these questions about money:

_____

_____

My Money Journal

(Jot down any money/business success you have after reading this book)

You can also send us a picture of your success! We will highlight your amazing hard work on social media and our website.
(Hello@AuthorCrystalMcLean.com)

GRANNY HAL'S FAMOUS LEMONADE

Be sure to get help from an adult

Makes about 8 cups
Prep Time: 10 mins

Ingredients:
- 3/4 cup fresh lemon juice (about 4-6 medium lemons)
- 1/4 cup fresh lime juice (about 2-3 limes)
- 1/4 cup fresh-squeezed orange juice (from 1 orange)
- 1 cup pure cane sugar
- 6 cups water (filtered tap water, if possible)

Instructions:

1. In a 2-quart sized pitcher, stir the lemon juice, lime juice, orange juice, and sugar together until the sugar is dissolved.
2. Add the water and stir to combine.
3. Serve over ice.

OOEY GOOEY COOKIES RECIPE

Be sure to get help from an adult

Makes about 18 large cookies
Prep Time: 10 mins

Ingredients:
- 1 ½ cups all-purpose flour
- 1 teaspoon baking soda
- ½ teaspoon salt
- ½ cup of unsalted butter (room temperature)
- ½ cup firmly packed light brown sugar
- 6 tablespoons granulated sugar
- 1 large egg
- 1 teaspoon vanilla extract
- 2 ¼ cups semi-sweet chocolate chips
- 1 ½ cups white chocolate chips

Instructions:
1. Preheat the oven to 350°F and use baking sheets lined with parchment paper. If you do not have parchment paper, use non-stick cooking spray.
2. In a medium mixing bowl, sift the flour, baking soda, and salt together.
3. In a separate bowl, use an electric mixer at medium speed to beat together the butter and sugars until smooth.

4. Add in the egg and vanilla and mix on low speed until fully mixed in.
5. Slowly add in the flour mixture and mix it in. Try not to overmix.
6. Add semi-sweet and white chocolate chips and stir with a wooden spoon. Try to make sure you don't overmix.
7. Chill dough for at least 2 hours.
8. Using a small ice cream scooper, drop the dough on the prepared baking sheets.
9. Bake until the cookies are lightly browned on top and around the edges. Make sure the tops feel firm when you touch them.
10. Let the cookies cool in the pan.
11. Now you have Ooey Gooey Cookies!

ENJOY!!..

About the Author

Crystal D. McLean is a native of Fayetteville, North Carolina. She is an alumna of Fayetteville State University, where she received her Bachelor of Science degree in Banking and Finance. Crystal is a proud supporter of her community and is involved in numerous volunteer and charitable organizations. She plays a direct, impactful role at her local assembly as the Youth Pastor along with her husband, Brandon McLean. As the proud mom of Harmony, she wanted to help other young people learn how to manage money. Her goal is to educate youth on financial awareness and give them tools to make financially sound decisions.

CPSIA information can be obtained
at www.ICGtesting.com
Printed in the USA
BVHW061439240422
635165BV00002B/127